TABLE OF CONTENTS

Novel-Ties® are printed on recycled paper.

For the Teacher

This reproducible study guide consists of lessons to use in conjunction with the novel *Tangerine*. Written in chapter-by-chapter format, the guide contains a synopsis, pre-reading activities, vocabulary and comprehension exercises, as well as extension activities to be used as follow-up to the novel.

In a homogeneous classroom, whole class instruction with one title is appropriate. In a heterogeneous classroom, reading groups should be formed: each group works on a different novel at its own reading level. Depending upon the length of time devoted to reading in the classroom, each novel, with its guide and accompanying lessons, may be completed in three to six weeks.

Begin using NOVEL-TIES for reading development by distributing the novel and a folder to each child. Distribute duplicated pages of the study guide for students to place in their folders. After examining the cover and glancing through the book, students can participate in several pre-reading activities. Vocabulary questions should be con- sidered prior to reading a chapter; all other work should be done after the chapter has been read. Comprehension questions can be answered orally or in writing. The classroom teacher should determine the amount of work to be assigned, always keeping in mind that readers must be nurtured and that the ultimate goal is encouraging students' love of reading.

The benefits of using NOVEL-TIES are numerous. Students read good literature in the original, rather than in abridged or edited form. The good reading habits, formed by practice in focusing on interpretive comprehension and literary techniques, will be transferred to the books students read independently. Passive readers become active, avid readers.

SYNOPSIS

For as long as he can remember, fourteen-year-old Paul Fisher has lived under the shadow of his older brother Erik, whose ambition to be a football star dominates his family's life. Paul's parents— particularly his father—dote on Erik, oblivious to Paul's own dream of playing goalie on a soccer team. To Paul, Erik is not a hero, but an arrogant bully. Paul fears his brother and suspects he is responsible for the mysterious accident years ago that left Paul legally blind and needing thick glasses.

The Fishers relocate to Lake Windsor Downs, a well-groomed gated community in Tangerine County, Florida. Hints of environmental nightmares lurk beneath the development's pristine veneer. Frequent thunderstorms ignite underground muck fires that burn perpetually in nearby fields and cast a shroud of smoke over the area.

Despite his visual impairment, Paul wins a spot on Lake Windsor Middle School's soccer team. He is dropped a few days later, however, because of his handicap. All seems hopeless until an environmental disaster causes school officials to suspend classes. Taking advantage of the situation, Paul enrolls in another school where he hopes to salvage his soccer dreams.

Tangerine Middle School sits in a poor part of town, where the "minorities are the majority." When Paul joins the soccer team, two of its star players, Tino Cruz and Victor Guzman, try to intimidate him. Paul proves himself on the soccer field, winning the boys' acceptance and respect. As his new soccer team scores a series of victories, Paul's friendships with his teammates grow. While visiting the citrus nursery owned by Tino's family, he meets Luis, Tino's older brother, a talented horticulturist whose quiet reverence for the land impresses Paul. At the nursery, Paul feels a harmonious balance struck between humanity and nature, whereas in his own community unsuccessful efforts to flood the muck fires have triggered an infestation of mosquitoes.

When Paul invites his new friends to his house, Erik and his uncouth friend Arthur taunt them and viciously assault Tino. The next day, Luis comes to Erik's football practice and challenges him to a fight. As they exchange harsh words, Arthur sneaks up behind Luis and smashes him unconscious with a blackjack. Paul, who has witnessed the entire incident from behind the bleachers, does and says nothing as his fear of Erik grows.

A week later, Paul hears the stunning news that Luis has died from an aneurysm. He suspects Arthur's blow with the blackjack is responsible. After a couple of agonizing days, wondering if anyone would believe his account of Luis's murder, Paul attends a school sports awards ceremony honoring Erik's team. In the middle of the ceremony, Tino and Victor stride into the gym and attack Erik and Arthur. School officials try to restrain Tino, but Paul hurls himself onto the coach and knocks him off balance, allowing Tino to break free and run. Moments later, Paul also manages to flee.

An hour later, Paul finds himself behind his house, cornered by Erik and Arthur. No longer afraid of his brother and his thuggish friend, Paul tells them that he witnessed the blow that killed Luis. As a maddened Erik screams at Paul and flees, an elusive memory comes into Paul's mind. It is a memory of Erik, pinning back five-year-old Paul's arms, prying open his eyelids, and letting a bully friend of his spray white paint into his eyes. When Paul confronts his parents with this memory, they tearfully confirm that it is the truth.

In the days that follow, Paul watches Erik's football dream unravel as a scandal strikes Erik's team, nullifying the team's victories and records set by its teammates. Then Paul's parents reveal their discovery that Erik and Arthur are guilty of a series of robberies in the housing development. Just when it appears that the boys may get off lightly, the police arrive to arrest Arthur and Erik for the murder of Luis.

Though Paul is expelled from all Tangerine County public schools for his role in the awards ceremony attack, it matters little to him. He is more concerned about writing a statement for the sheriff in which he expresses how much Luis meant to everyone and how little Erik contributed to the world.

On a cold Florida morning, Paul's father drives him to his new school. As they pass rows and rows of citrus groves, Paul leans his head out the car window and breathes in the cold, clear, sweet-scented air as he anticipates a future free of lies and fear.

PRE-READING ACTIVITIES

1. Preview the book by reading the title and the author's name and by looking at the illustration on the cover of the book. Also notice the quotation inside the book from The Doors song, "The Soft Parade."

   Successful hills are here to stay.
   Everything must be this way.

   What do you think the book will be about? Do you think it will be realistic fiction or fantasy? What do you think the words in the quotation suggest? Why do you think the author chose to quote these particular lines?

2. What role do you think parents play in determining how their teenagers act outside the home? What role do you think their friends and classmates play in the way they behave?

3. Paul, the main character in the novel, lives in a housing development in which strict rules ensure that the houses maintain a consistent appearance. Everything —even the mailboxes and the color of the houses—must conform to certain standards. Why do you think some people find this kind of community appealing? Would you like this kind of community?

4. Many environmental problems plague the community in which Paul lives. What kinds of stresses might a housing development place upon its natural environment? What would be an effective way to deal with these problems?

5. Are there any environmental problems in your community? Are they being addressed or are they being ignored? Why might a community want to hide its environmental problems? How can a community mobilize to address these problems?

6. Sibling rivalry refers to competition between brothers and sisters. If you have brothers or sisters, in what ways do you compete with one another? Why do siblings compete? At what point does sibling rivalry become unhealthy competition?

7. High school football players are often idolized by their peers and community. What are the qualities that make a person truly heroic? Do heroic acts always conform to the wishes of the community? Should they? Why or why not?

8. The pressure to excel can be formidable for a high school athlete. A player's performance can win him or her publicity, scholarship offers from prestigious colleges, and perhaps an opportunity to have a career in professional sports. Is this kind of pressure good for high school athletics? Why or why not? How does good sportsmanship fare under this pressure?

9. Sometimes, people keep secrets to protect the ones they love from a painful truth. What kinds of secrets might parents keep from their children? Under what circumstances do family secrets become harmful?

10. **Cooperative Learning Activity:** Form debating teams to argue the following question: should a student with a handicap be permitted to play on a school team?

Pre-Reading Activities (cont.)

11. In the following Anticipation Guide, place a check in the "Before Reading" column next to each of the items with which you agree. When you finish reading the book, return to the guide and place a check next to each item in the "After Reading" column with which you now agree. Did the book change any of your opinions?

Statement	Before Reading	After Reading
1. A healthy environment depends on a delicate balance. When one element is disturbed, the entire environment suffers.		
2. With community involvement, environmental problems can be easily solved.		
3. It is possible to remember events that occurred in early childhood.		
4. Memories of terrible events can be totally repressed.		
5. Parents have the obligation to shield their children from unpleasant memories, even if it is necessary to lie.		
6. "The truth will set you free." It is always better to reveal the truth and not lie.		
7. Violent children need discipline and professional help.		
8. If violent children receive love and patience at home, little discipline is needed.		
9. It is better to attend a school in an upper class neighborhood than one in a poor or working class neighborhood.		
10. Students with a physical handicap should not be allowed to play on school teams.		

PART I: PAGES 1 - 33 [Harcourt edition]

Vocabulary: Draw a line from each word on the left to its definition on the right. Then use the numbered words to fill in the blanks in the sentences below.

1. sprinted	a. surface layer of earth containing grass and its roots; turf
2. sod	b. movable
3. dominant	c. ran at full speed; dashed
4. portable	d. abnormally preoccupied
5. constitutes	e. weakened; disabled
6. impaired	f. most important; supreme
7. penalty	g. player on a football team who calls the signals and directs the offensive plays
8. obsessed	h. punishment; fine
9. quarterback	i. makes up; forms

. . . .

1. He was so ____________________ with the idea of winning the tournament that he could think of nothing else for weeks on end.
2. My parents bought me this laptop computer because it is lightweight and ____________________.
3. Her vision was ____________________ when dust blew into her eyes.
4. I ____________________ the short distance from the car to the house so I wouldn't get soaked in the downpour.
5. The ____________________ on my brother's football team is well known for directing complicated plays that often confuse the opposing team.
6. The ____________________ in our yard is overgrown with crabgrass.
7. His involvement in the robbery ____________________ a federal offense.
8. The ____________________ feeling among the members of the jury was that the defendant was innocent.
9. "For your role in this terrible crime," the judge declared, "the ____________________ shall be life imprisonment."

Part I: Pages 1 - 33 (cont.)

Read to learn about the new community where Paul's parents chose to live.

Questions:

1. Why were Paul and his mother leaving Houston?
2. What evidence showed that Paul feared and distrusted his older brother, Erik?
3. How did the landscape change as Paul and his mother entered Tangerine County?
4. How did Paul react when his father started talking about the "Erik Fisher Football Dream"? Why did Paul have this reaction?
5. Why did muck fires burn in the fields surrounding Lake Windsor Downs? How did these fires affect the environment of the development? Why was Mrs. Fisher upset by this news?
6. Why was Paul impressed with Mike Costello?
7. Why was Mrs. Fisher disappointed when she first examined Lake Windsor Middle School? How did Paul feel about it?
8. Why was Paul confident that he would get onto the soccer team?

Questions for Discussion:

1. Do you think Paul was justified in resenting his brother?
2. Why do you think Paul became angry when his mother informed his school of his visual impairment? If you were in Paul's situation, how do you think you would react?
3. Do you think the developers of Lake Windsor Downs were honest with potential buyers?
4. Would you be able to accept the environmental conditions at Lake Windsor Downs?

Literary Devices:

I. *Point of View* — The point of view in literature refers to the voice telling the story. It could be a character or the author narrating the story.

From whose point of view is this story told?

____

How does this point of view draw you into the story? What are its advantages? What are its limitations?

____

____

____

Part I: Pages 1 - 33 (cont.)

II. *Simile* — A simile is a figure of speech that compares two unlike objects or ideas using the words "like" or "as." For example:

> We sat in the beating rain noise for a few minutes, then it abruptly stopped, like some annoying little kid had stopped banging on a pan.

What is being compared?

____

How does the comparison help you experience the scene?

____

____

III. *Irony* — Irony refers to a situation that is the opposite of what is expected. What is ironic about Mr. Fisher's occupation and his move to Tangerine County?

____

____

Literary Element: Setting

Setting in literature refers to the time and place in which the events occur. What is the setting of *Tangerine*?

____

What comment do you think the author is making about the setting he chose?

____

____

____

In what ways might the setting be important in this novel?

____

____

____

Writing Activity:

Paul struggled with the feeling that his parents were more concerned with his brother's life than with his own. Have you ever struggled with similar feelings? Have you ever felt that a sibling's or friend's accomplishments cast a shadow over your own achievements? Write about this experience and tell how you dealt with it.

PART I: PAGES 33 - 61

Vocabulary: Use one word from the Word Box to replace the underlined word or phrase in each of the following sentences. Write the word on the line below the sentence.

WORD BOX			
benefactor	eclipse	perimeter	slouching
calisthenics	funneling	singed	torque

1. He lost the race because his car did not have enough force to make it turn to take the sharp curves quickly.

 ____

2. I slightly burned my eyebrows when I leaned too close to the flame.

 ____

3. We had to wear special glasses when we watched the overshadowing of the sun by the moon.

 ____

4. The artist was fortunate to have an enthusiastic person who gave her help supporting her work.

 ____

5. A chain-link fence marked the outer boundary of the athletic field.

 ____

6. The midpack racers have reached the last mile and will soon be moving to the central point through the finish line.

 ____

7. Our coach has us do exercises to help us build strong, trim bodies.

 ____

8. I am very comfortable standing in a drooping posture, but my mother always tells me to stand up straight.

 ____

Part I: Pages 33 - 61 (cont.)

Read to find out why Mrs. Fischer calls a meeting at her house.

Questions:

1. Why was the story of the eclipse important to Paul? Why did it puzzle him?
2. Why did Paul excuse Kerri Gardner from the duty of guiding him around the school?
3. Why did Erik choose Arthur to be his friend? How would Arthur profit from the relationship?
4. How did the Homeowners' Association try to control the appearance of the development? Why did Paul's mother appreciate the Association's efforts?
5. Why did Paul think the Donnellys' house had been struck repeatedly by lightning? How did Joey respond to this theory?
6. Why was Paul certain he had landed the job of goalie for the middle school soccer team?
7. Why did Paul's mother hold a meeting of football parents? How did various members of the community respond to her suggestion?

Questions for Discussion:

1. What are the advantages and disadvantages of living in a gated community such as Lake Windsor Downs?
2. Why do you think Erik didn't drive?
3. Why do you think all the children in Paul's classes seemed to lack energy?
4. What is your opinion of Coach Walski's policy of allowing only the most capable players to play in the soccer games? If you were to recommend changes to this policy, what would you recommend?
5. Compare Paul's reaction to the news of Mike Costello's death to Erik and Arthur's reaction. What would you have done if you had witnessed the boys joking about Mike's death?
6. What seem to be the common themes among Paul's memories?
7. Why do you think there was unspoken hostility between Mr. and Mrs. Fisher after the meeting that was held at their home?

Part I: Pages 33 - 61 (cont.)

Literary Device: Personification

Personification is a literary device in which an author grants lifelike qualities to nonhuman objects, animals, or ideas. For example:

> Now, you could bring back those developers, and the construction guys, and the engineers, and ask them to point out where the highest spot around here used to be. Not one of them would know. But the lightning knows. It hits right where it's always hit.

What is being personified?

___

How does this use of personification help you understand Paul's state of mind?

___

___

Literary Element: Contrast

Contrasting elements in a novel serve to highlight the characteristics of each. Compare and contrast the following pairs of elements. Notice other pairs as you continue to read.

Paul	——	Erik
soccer	——	football
Mike Costello	——	Arthur
Ads for Lake Windsor Downs	——	Reality at Windsor Lake Downs

Writing Activity:

Imagine you are Paul and write a letter to a friend in Houston in which you describe your new community and some of the people you have met. Also, convey your thoughts and feelings about Lake Windsor Downs.

PART I: PAGES 61 - 94

Vocabulary: Word analogies are equations in which the first pair of words has the same relationship as the second pair of words. For example: TIRE is to CAR as KNEE is to BODY. The relationship of both pairs of words is that of part to whole. Choose the best word from the Word Box to complete each of the analogies below.

WORD BOX			
commotion	eligible	obituary	partitioned
elated	migrant	osprey	vaulting

1. BIRTH is to BIRTH ANNOUNCEMENT as DEATH is to ________________.
2. ________________ is to UNSUITABLE as JOLLY is to MISERABLE.
3. WANDERER is to ________________ as SUPERVISOR is to OVERSEER.
4. BEAGLE is to DOG as ________________ is to BIRD.
5. HAPPY is to ________________ as UNINTERESTED is to BORED.
6. ELEVATED is to LOWERED as UNIFIED is to ________________.
7. ________________ is to CALM as INTERIOR is to EXTERIOR.
8. LEAPING is to ________________ as RUNNING is to SPRINTING.

Read to find out why Paul's dream of playing soccer might come to pass.

Questions:

1. Why did Paul blame his mother when he was dropped from the soccer team? Compare Mr. and Mrs. Fisher's responses to the situation.
2. Why did the conversations at Mike's wake surprise Paul?
3. Why was Paul both comforted and troubled by the sight of the tangerine packing plant and the migrant workers' houses?
4. At the carnival, why did Joey hustle Paul away from the group of boys with the soccer ball?
5. Why didn't Paul go on any of the rides at the carnival?
6. Why was Paul surprised by the television report on the sinkhole disaster at his school? How did the report differ from his direct experience of the disaster?
7. Why was Mr. Fisher promoted as a result of the sinkhole disaster? Why was he worried about the promotion?
8. Why was Paul elated about the possibility of transferring to Tangerine Middle School?

Part I: Pages 61 - 94 (cont.)

Questions for Discussion:

1. Do you think Paul would be a liability on the soccer field? Do you think the principal was being fair to Paul?
2. Do you think Coach Warner cared about the well-being of his players?
3. Why was Paul pleased with his own response to the sinkhole disaster? What did his actions indicate about his character? How do you think you would respond in a similar situation?
4. Do you think there are any overlooked environmental problems in your community that could lead to disaster?

Literary Devices:

I. *Symbolism* — A symbol in literature is an object, event, or character that represents an idea or a set of ideas. What do you think the freak show exhibit of the Boy Who Never Grew symbolized for Paul?

____

____

II. *Irony* — What is ironic about Paul identifying the people who vandalized the Wonders of the World Exhibit at the carnival? Why is it ironic that none of the other soccer players were able to do so?

____

____

____

Writing Activity:

Imagine that you are a newspaper reporter for the local Tangerine County newspaper. You are covering the sinkhole disaster at Lake Windsor Middle School. Write an article about this event that would appear in the paper. You might wish to include interviews or quotations from some of the people involved. Be sure to include the important *who, what, why, when,* and *where* of the incident.

PART 2: PAGES 97 - 124

Vocabulary: Use the context to determine the meaning of the underlined word in each of the following sentences. Then compare your definition with a dictionary definition.

1. The costume designer spent many hours shopping for <u>vintage</u> clothes at second-hand stores.
   Your definition ______________________________
   Dictionary definition ______________________________
2. The shopowners bring down steel gates at night to protect their property from <u>vandalism</u>.
   Your definition ______________________________
   Dictionary definition ______________________________
3. Their conversation began as light <u>banter</u> but soon shifted to mean-spirited insults.
   Your definition ______________________________
   Dictionary definition ______________________________
4. Excitement among the spectators built to a <u>frenzy</u> as the game approached its tie-breaking point.
   Your definition ______________________________
   Dictionary definition ______________________________
5. He tried to stop himself, but the <u>momentum</u> of the fall sent him crashing into the wall.
   Your definition ______________________________
   Dictionary definition ______________________________

Read to learn how Paul became part of the team.

Questions:

1. How did Paul's visual impairment help him adjust to the tough students at Tangerine Middle School?
2. Why was Paul content to play backup for the goalie?
3. Why did Paul feel hopeful after his first day of school at Tangerine Middle School?
4. How did Paul handle Victor's efforts to intimidate him? What might have happened if he had chosen a more aggressive response?
5. Why was Joey disappointed in himself when Eric and Arthur teased him about his brother's death? How did Paul comfort Joey?
6. Why were the War Eagles a better team than the Palmetto Whippoorwills?
7. How did Victor let Paul know that he considered him part of the team?

Part 2: Pages 97 - 124 (cont.)

Questions for Discussion:

1. Do you think Paul's mother should have "lost" the IEP forms?
2. Do you think Paul should have revealed to Victor, Tino, and Hernandez that he was the informant?
3. Do you think it is a good idea for Joey to join Paul at Tangerine Middle School? What might be the advantages and disadvantages for each boy?

Literary Device: Dramatic Irony

Dramatic irony, a device used more often in plays than in novels, occurs when the audience or the reader has information which one or more of the characters lack. What is the dramatic irony implicit in the scene in which Victor describes how he and his buddies ended up in jail after attending the carnival?

___

___

Literary Element: Setting

The setting in literature refers to the time and place in which the events occur. Use the Venn diagram below to compare Lake Windsor Middle School to Tangerine Middle School. Write about the qualities they share in the overlapping part of the circles.

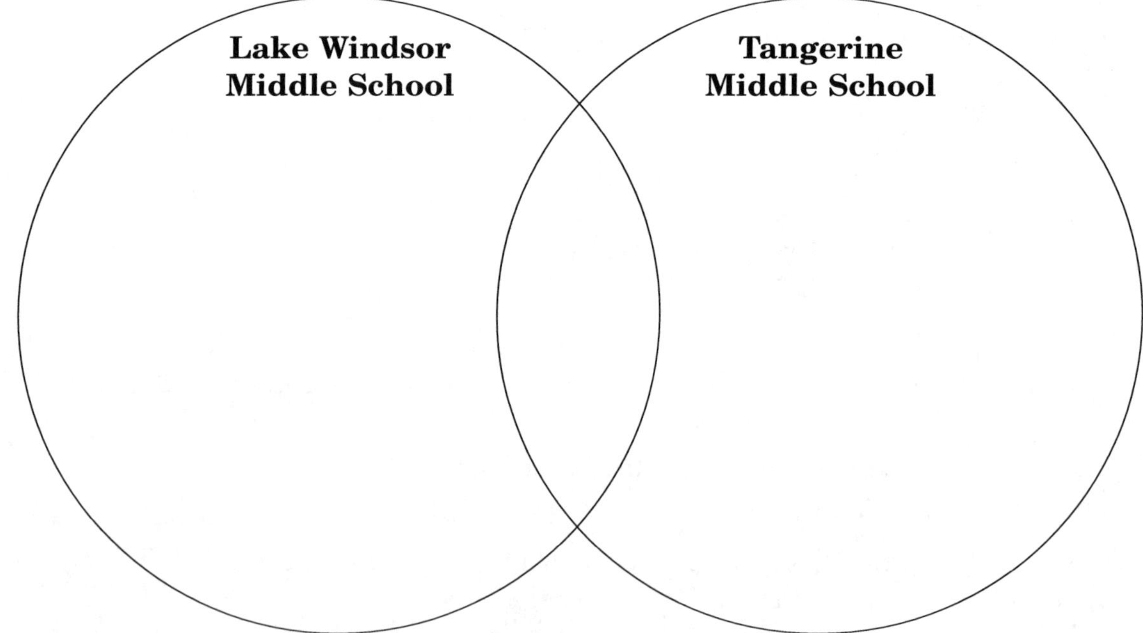

Writing Activity:

Write about a time when you witnessed an act of cruelty. Describe this situation and tell how you responded to it.

PART 2: PAGES 124 - 155

Vocabulary: Use the words in the Word Box and the clues below to complete the crossword puzzle.

WORD BOX				
adjourn	decoy	fumigate	prominence	sulking
condemned	dilapidated	initiation	punt	swiveled

Across

1. shabby; neglected
4. turned; pivoted
6. suspend business for a time
8. expose to fumes in order to kill vermin
9. declared to be evil or guilty

Down

2. ceremony or rite by which someone is introduced to something
3. artificial object or person used to lure or trap prey
4. showing resentment by withdrawing and refusing to speak
5. state of being noticeable or conspicuous
7. type of kick in which the ball is dropped from the hands and kicked before it strikes the ground.

Part 2: Pages 124 - 155 (cont.)

Questions:

1. How did Eric's parents try to relieve the humiliation of the fake kick?
2. How did Paul compare himself to Shandra as a goalie?
3. Why was Victor taken out of the second half of the game with Kinnow? How did he help his team win the game?
4. Why was Paul shocked when he scored a goal?
5. Why was Maya confused when Mrs. Fisher offered her words of encouragement?
6. Why did Joey turn down Mrs. Fisher's invitation to stay at the Fisher home while his own was being fumigated? How did Paul compare his home to Joey's?
7. How did Paul learn that Joey was prejudiced?
8. How had the Homeowners' Association tried to solve the problem of the muck fires? How had these efforts proven to be unsuccessful?

Questions for Discussion:

1. Do you think that Erik will make someone pay for his humiliation at the opening day game? How do you think Erik might do this?
2. Why do you think Paul and Joey's parents failed to attend soccer games for Tangerine Middle School?
3. Why do you think Joey had a harder time dealing with the boys on the soccer team than Paul?
4. Why do you think Shandra ran away when she saw the *Tangerine Times* van and photographer? Why did Hernando, Tino, and Mano try to divert the reporter?
5. Why do you think Tino became angry when Joey suggested that he prepare the group's report on his computer?

Science Connection:

Notice the chain of dire ecological events in Tangerine County that began with the construction of homes over a lignite field, creating muck fires, which in turn required flooding. This led to a mosquito infestation which contributed to disease and the death of infants. Trace the path of one ecological mistake in your community to its possible or actual chain of consequences and its ultimate tragedies.

Writing Activity:

Imagine you are Paul. Write a letter to Joey in which you tell him what you think of his attitude toward the students at Tangerine Middle School.

PART 2: PAGES 155 - 199

Vocabulary: Use one word from the Word Box to replace the underlined word or phrase in each of the following sentences. Write the word on the line below the sentence.

WORD BOX			
boycott	congregated	peripheral	reverence
cleats	horticulture	retaliate	scion

1. The crowd gathered in the lobby before entering the auditorium.

   ____

2. As the firstborn male child in a wealthy family, John would undoubtedly inherit a great deal of money.

   ____

3. We will refuse to do business with that store because we disapprove of the unfair way they treat their employees.

   ____

4. As I was walking through the woods, I used the outer part of my field of vision to watch for animals.

   ____

5. The coach requires that we wear shoes equipped with spikes on the soles so that our shoes will grip the ground when we run.

   ____

6. The professor was regarded with awed respect by generations of his students.

   ____

7. He was wise to resist the urge to get revenge against those who had tried to hurt his business.

   ____

8. The landscape designer spent several years studying the science and art of growing plants.

   ____

Part 2: Pages 155 - 199 (cont.)

Read to find out what happened at the soccor match between the Tangerine War Eagles and the Lake Windsor team.

Questions:

1. Why was Paul worried about seeing Tino? How did he win Tino's respect?
2. Why were termites infesting the houses in the development? Why was fumigation only a temporary remedy?
3. What fragment of memory was triggered for Paul as he watched the white cloud of mosquito spray billow over the backyard?
4. Why did Paul believe that he could "see" better than his parents?
5. Why did Paul feel that his season with the War Eagles was the greatest thing that ever happened to him?
6. How did Tino feel about his brother Luis? How did this compare with Paul's feeling about Erik?
7. Why did the Tangerine War Eagles regard the Lake Windsor soccer team as its archenemy?
8. According to Paul, why were his soccer teammates impressed with the housing developments that they passed on the way to the game?
9. How did Coach Bright refocus her team after a player on the opposing team punched Victor?

Questions for Discussion:

1. What do you think Arthur scooped from the dashboard of his car?
2. Why do you think Paul continued to have flashes of unexpected memories? What do you think they mean?
3. Why do you think the Lake Windsor players and fans were shocked by the War Eagles' war cry?
4. Do you think Coach Walski was being fair when he tried to declare Paul ineligible to play in the game? What did his behavior indicate about his character?
5. Why do you think Paul chose to ride the bus all the way back to Tangerine Middle School after the game?

Literary Devices:

I. *Allusion* — An allusion in literature is a reference to an important person, place, thing, or event. What is being referred to in the following allusion?

> Wayne spotted the blue tents along Joey's street. "Look at that, now," he said. "Y'all are having a regular nine plagues of Egypt over here, aren't you?"

____

In what way did this allusion reflect Wayne's attitude?

____

Part 2: Pages 155 - 199 (cont.)

II. *Simile* — A simile is a figure of speech in which two unlike objects are compared using the words “like” or “as.” What is being compared in the following simile?

> I saw a billowing white cloud enter the backyard, like
> an angel of death.

Why is this an apt comparison?

Science Connection:

Do some research to learn more about tree grafting. Find out why it is sometimes advantageous to graft the branches of one plant to the root stock of another. Learn about successes and failures in the field.

Literary Element: Characterization

We learn about characters in literature from what they say, what they do, and from what other characters say about them. How was Luis's character revealed at the Tangerine nursery?

Writing Activities:

1. Write about a time when you admitted doing something you felt was wrong. What happened as a result of your admission?
2. Write about a time when you played an important part in a group effort.

PART 3: PAGES 203 - 230

Vocabulary: Synonyms are words with similar meanings. Draw a line from each word in column A to its synonym in column B. Then use the words in column A to fill in the blanks in the sentences below.

A	B
1. paralyzed	a. rude
2. mesmerized	b. decrepit
3. insolent	c. plod
4. contorted	d. hypnotized
5. trudge	e. trash
6. debris	f. immobilized
7. rickety	g. twisted

. . . .

1. It is important to clean up the ____________________ before you leave a picnic site.
2. The deer became ____________________ with fear as it faced the oncoming headlights.
3. It was difficult to ____________________ even a short distance in the deep snow.
4. The young boy was punished for being ____________________ to his parents.
5. After years of neglect, we decided to replace the ____________________ old fence.
6. The patient became ____________________ as her eyes followed a moving beam of light.
7. The batter's face ____________________ with rage when he realized that the pitcher was trying to hit him with the baseball.

Read to find out what happens when a freeze hits the tangerine trees.

Questions:

1. Why did Erik assault Tino?
2. Why did Arthur assault Luis?
3. Why were so many students absent from school when the freeze hit Tangerine County?
4. Why did Luis spray water on the citrus trees?
5. Why did Luis hesitate when Paul offered to help fight the freeze? How did Paul convince him of his good will?

Part 3: Pages 203 - 230 (cont.)

6. Why did the Cruz family try to avoid chopping down their "lightning trees?' Why did they have to chop down a few of them during the freeze?
7. Contrast the way people in Lake Windsor Downs responded to the freeze with the way the farming families in Tangerine responded to it.

Questions for Discussion:

1. Do you think the confrontation between Tino and Erik at the Fisher's house could have been avoided? Was Erik's response justified?
2. Why do you think Erik looked sorrowful or fearful after he assaulted Tino? If you had been present, what would you have done?
3. Why do you think Paul couldn't tell his parents about Erik's assault of Tino? Do you think he should have talked to them about this?
4. Why do you think Paul's grandparents avoided the subject of Erik's football dream?
5. Why do you think Shandra's picture was missing from the newspaper photo of the All-County Middle School Soccer Team?
6. How would you compare the Cruz's regard for the land with that of the Homeowners' Association? Why do you think this difference of attitude exists?

Literary Devices:

I. *Simile* — What is being compared in the following simile?

> I watched that hand [Erik's hand], mesmerized. I watched it move like a snake—a slow, casual snake hand—with a gold varsity ring on one finger.

___

What does this reveal about Erik's character?

___

___

II. *Metaphor* — A metaphor is a figure of speech in which a comparison is suggested or implied. For example:

> That turned out to be our last moment of peace. For the next twelve hours, we waged a fierce and increasingly desperate battle to save the Cruz family's trees.

What is being compared?

___

Why is this an apt comparison?

___

___

Part 3: Pages 203 - 230 (cont.)

III. *Irony* — What was ironic about the appearance of the new grove on the night of the freeze?

____

____

Literary Element: Conflict

Conflict in literature refers to the clash of opposing forces. There are three major forms of conflict. Use the chart below to record each type of conflict as it appears in the novel. Add to the chart as you continue to read the book.

Conflicts	Examples
Person *vs.* Person/Society	
Person *vs.* Nature	
Person *vs.* Self (inner struggle)	

Writing Activity:

Imagine a scene in which Paul expresses his frustration toward his parents who refuse to see Erik clearly. Write dialogue that could be spoken by Paul, Mrs. Fisher, and Mr. Fisher. Perhaps Erik interrupts their argument. You may perform your scene with classmates for the class.

PART 3: PAGES 230 - 265

Vocabulary: Choose the best word from the Word Box to complete each of the analogies below.

WORD BOX		
bogus	prostrate	sterile
mirage	pummel	veered

1. DELIRIUM is to MADNESS as HALLUCINATION is to ___________________.
2. GENUINE is to ___________________ as CHEAP is to EXPENSIVE.
3. JUMPED is to LEAPED as SWERVED is to ___________________.
4. ___________________ is to PRONE as STIFF is to RIGID.
5. SMOOTH is to ROUGH as ___________________ is to FILTHY.
6. ___________________ is to AGGRESSION as HUG is to AFFECTION.

Read to find out about the truth in Paul's family.

Questions:

1. Why had Mr. Fisher deleted some colleges from Erik's "Scholarship Offers" file?
2. How did the freeze alleviate some of the environmental problems of Lake Windsor Downs?
3. Why did Paul resist sharing his suspicions about the cause of Luis's death with his mother?
4. Why was Paul sure that Erik and Arthur were responsible for Luis's death?
5. How did Luis's family know the truth about the cause of his death? Why did their understanding of the truth seem mysterious to Paul?
6. Why was Paul no longer afraid when Erik and Arthur threatened him with the baseball bat? What weapon of his own did he use to combat Erik?
7. Why had Paul's parents lied to him about the cause of his visual impairment? How did Paul convince them this was a terrible decision?

Part 3: Pages 230 - 265 (cont.)

Questions for Discussion:

1. Why do you think Mr. Fisher seemed "unglued" at the meeting of the Homeowners' Association?
2. Why do you think the Homeowners' Association had difficulty believing that the ospreys were the reason the koi disappeared from the development's pond?
3. Do you think Paul shared any of the guilt for Luis's death?
4. Why do you think Paul told the little boy on the bicycle that the boy's parents had been lying to him? What did this reveal about Paul's state of mind?
5. Do you think Paul expressed his grief over Luis's death in an appropriate manner?
6. Why do you think the usher at Senior Awards Night referred to Erik as "Mr. Generosity"?
7. What do you predict will happen to Erik?

Literary Device: Flashback

A flashback is a device that an author uses to interrupt a story in order to relate an event that happened at an earlier time. What past event did the author relate?

___

___

Why did the author use a flashback?

___

___

Why was the information in the flashback important?

___

___

Writing Activities:

1. Imagine you are Paul. Write a letter to Erik, telling him what you have learned about the true cause of your visual impairment.
2. Now imagine you are Erik and write a response to Paul's letter.

PART 3: PAGES 266 - 303

Vocabulary: Draw a line from each word on the left to its meaning on the right. Then use the numbered words to fill in the blanks in the sentences below.

1.	nullify	a.	brusquely; tersely
2.	immortality	b.	restoration of something to its rightful owner
3.	restitution	c.	cancel out; invalidate
4.	unanimous	d.	mildly or submissively
5.	ransacked	e.	plundered; searched carefully with the intention to rob
6.	meekly	f.	unending existence; lasting fame
7.	compelled	g.	having the agreement of all
8.	curtly	h.	caused to do by overwhelming pressure

• •

1. The dog hung its head ____________________ when it was scolded for chewing the table leg.
2. The mess and confusion that met our eyes when we entered the apartment suggested that it had been ____________________ by robbers.
3. The examiners will ____________________ the score on your test if you are caught cheating.
4. "Either pay attention in my class or leave," the professor said ________________.
5. The athlete believed his ____________________ would be assured once he won a gold medal.
6. To convict the defendant the jury had to reach a(n) ____________________ decision.
7. When the witness learned he could go to jail for withholding evidence, he felt ____________________ to tell the court everything he knew about the robbery.
8. She hoped to make ____________________ for the stolen money by returning it immediately.

> Read to find out whether Paul and his family will live a life without lies.

Questions:

1. Why did Antoine tell Paul not to spend his life hiding under the bleachers? How did Paul react to this advice?
2. Why did Antoine's confession nullify his team's victories? How did this confession affect Erik's record?

PART 3: PAGES 266 - 303

3. Why had Antoine initially chosen to lie about where he lived?
4. Why was Mr. Donnelly unable to feel proud about retaining his record for "the most passing yards in a single game?"
5. Why did Paul question his father's eyesight when he had expressed shock over Antoine's true address when people called?
6. Why did Mrs. Fisher call a meeting at her house?
7. Why did Mr. Fisher want everyone at the meeting to agree to the restitution plan?
8. Why weren't Paul's grandparents surprised when they learned the news about Erik?
9. Why was Paul confident he would be regarded with respect and fear at St. Anthony's?
10. How did Mr. and Mrs. Fisher learn the complete truth about their son's actions? What else do you think they learned?

Questions for Discussion:

1. Do you think it is legitimate for high school students to lie about their addresses in order to attend a school of their choice?
2. Do you think the county should have rescinded the scores and individual records of the Lake Windsor Downs football team?
3. Do you think Paul should have told the police about Arthur and Erik's involvement in Luis's death? Should he have acted sooner?
4. Do you agree with Grandpop that the Fishers should have dealt more seriously with Erik years ago? How do you think they should have dealt with him?
5. Why did Theresa have renewed respect for Paul? Do you think it was justified?
6. Do you think Paul's sacrifice on Luis's behalf was worth it when balanced against the punishment he received?

Literary Devices:

I. *Irony* — Why was it ironic when Shandra said to Paul, "You don't have to live a lie everyday of your natural-born life, do you"?

____

____

II. *Symbolism* — What did Paul's new clothes and the purging of his old wardrobe symbolize?

____

____

Part 3: Pages 266 - 303 (cont.)

III. *Metaphor* — What is being compared in the following metaphor?

> . . . I heard Erik pacing back and forth, back and forth, in the cage that he had made himself.

___

What does this reveal about Erik's state of mind?

___

___

IV. *Analogy* — An analogy in literature is the comparison of two or more similar objects so as to suggest that if they are alike in certain respects, they will probably be alike in other ways as well. How was Lake Windsor Downs with its hidden environmental problems analogous to the Fisher family?

___

___

___

___

Literary Element: Mood

Mood in literature refers to the feeling the reader gets from the story. What is the mood of the last paragraph of the story? How does the author use setting to express mood?

> Soon the road narrowed to two lanes and we were surrounded by the groves, surrounded by the beauty of it all. I stared through the window at the endless rows of trees—orange, tangerine, lemon—flying past us on either side. I rolled down the window and let it all in. The air was clear and cold. And the car immediately filled up with that scent, the scent of a golden dawn.

___

___

___

___

Writing Activity:

Imagine you are Paul six months after Erik's arrest. Write a journal entry describing how your life has changed.

CLOZE ACTIVITY

The following passage is taken from page one hundred twenty-two. Read it through completely. Then go back and fill in each blank with a word that makes sense. Afterward, you may compare your words with those of the author.

Victor was in my face immediately, his finger nearly stabbing through my chest. He screamed, "If we lose this game, ______________[1] dead!"

A minute later I got another ______________[2] to shoot the ball, but one Palmetto ______________[3] knocked me down and the other kicked ______________[4] away. I started to get up, but ______________[5] I could, the fullback stretched out my ______________[6] from my face, scooped up a handful ______________[7] mud, and smeared it in my eyes. ______________[8] *my eyes*! I went berserk!

Before he ______________[9] get away, I scrambled up and jumped ______________[10] his back. I brought him down and ______________[11] punching at him blindly, the way I'd ______________[12] Tino do it. A whistle started blowing, ______________[13] soon I felt the coach's big hands ______________[14] me off him and dragging me away.

______________[15] stood next to the coach for the ______________[16] of the game, mud all over me, ______________[17] pouring out of my nose, tears pouring ______________[18] of my eyes. I heard my teammates ______________,[19] so I took off my goggles, cleaned ______________[20] the best I could, and put them ______________[21] on.

Through the blurry plastic lenses, I ______________[22] Victor take the ball through the Palmetto ______________[23] like a wild bull. He fought off ______________[24] nasty tackle, and then another. He lowered ______________[25] shoulder at the fullback and crashed into ______________.[26] The Palmetto goalie slid at him, but ______________[27] was too quick. He pushed the ball ______________[28] the right and vaulted over him. Then ______________[29] kicked it into the open goal. It was 1-1.

POST-READING ACTIVITIES

1. Return to the Anticipation Guide that you began in the Pre-Reading Activities on page four of this study guide. Fill in column three and discuss with your classmates any opinions that you changed due to reading this book.
2. Return to the conflict chart you began on page twenty-two. Be sure that you have completed the chart. Compare your chart with those of your classmates.
3. Imagine that Erik's parents had held him accountable when he injured Paul's eyes. In what ways do you think this story would have been different?
4. Imagine that you are going to make this book into a film. Are there any changes or additions you would make? Are there any scenes that should be omitted? How would you deal with Paul's computerized diary entries? Who do you think might play the roles of Paul, Erik, and Tino? Do you think this book would translate well into a movie?
5. Did you find the ending of the novel effective? Why or why not? How would you have ended the novel?
6. Paul hates and fears his brother. Is Erik truly the cause of Paul's problems? What do you think caused Erik's problems?
7. A theme is a central idea or an author's message that is carried throughout a story. Work with a partner to trace the following themes as they appear throughout the novel:
   - Family relationships and dysfunction are complex.
   - Bigotry and discrimination lead to disastrous consequences.
   - Standing up for the truth, despite personal cost, may be painful.
   - One must be accountable for one's actions.
   - How we treat the environment parallels human relationships.
8. Write a paragraph about each of the following main characters, briefly describing what you think each might be doing ten years after the time of the story:

Paul	Erik	Tino
Victor	Arthur	Mrs. Fisher
Antoine	Shandra	Joey

9. Paul lives in a place where the homes are surrounded by smoldering muck fires, infested by termites, and poisoned with insecticide. Even his school is sucked underground by a flooded sinkhole. How is setting used in this story to serve as a metaphor for Paul's inner life? Work with a partner to find passages in the book in which the setting plays a critical role and discuss how it reflects Paul's personal situation.

Post-Reading Activities (cont.)

10. Are there any housing developments in your area? Find out about the kinds of natural settings they are built upon, how old they are, what kinds of environ- mental problems they may have faced, and the solutions residents have tried to solve these problems.

11. **Science Connection:** When mosquitoes infest Lake Windsor Downs, the Homeowners' Association sprays the development with insecticide. Research the pros and cons of using poisonous substances to exterminate pests. Find out about the kinds of non-toxic alternatives that are available. Form debating teams to argue which method is preferable.

12. Interview students who are active in team sports at your school. Find out what kinds of issues they have encountered, such as fair rotation of players, accep- tance of co-ed teams, parental involvement or apathy, competition, team cooperation, and violence. How are their stories similar to those of Paul and Erik?

13. **Literature Circle:** Have a literature circle discussin in which you tell your personal reactions to *Tangerine*. Here are some questions and sentence starters to help your literature circle begin a discussion.
    - How are you like Paul? How are you different?
    - Do you think the characters in the novel are realistic? Why or why not?
    - Which character did you like the most? The least?
    - Who else should read this novel? Why?
    - What questions would you like to ask the author of this novel?
    - It was not fair when. . .
    - I would have liked to see. . .
    - I didn't understand. . .
    - Paul learned that. . .

SUGGESTIONS FOR FURTHER READING

Bennett, James W. *Blue Star Rapture*. Simon Pulse.
Bowler, Tim. *Midget*. Simon Pulse.
Crutchner, Chris. *Ironman*. Greenwillow.
Dygard, Thomas J. *Game Plan*. Puffin.
Fraustino, Lisa Rowe. *Ash: A Novel*. Orchard Books
Hiaasen, Carl. *Flush*. Yearling.
* ____________. *Hoot*. Yearling.
Hughes, Dean. *Team Picture*. Aladdin.
Lynch, Chris. *Iceman*. HarperCollins.
____________. *Shadow Boxer*. HarperCollins.
Manes, Stephen. *An Almost Perfect Game*. Apple.
* Myers, Walter Dean. *Monster*. Amistad.
__________________. *Slam!* Scholastic.
Neenan, Colin. *In Your Dreams*. Graphia.
Oppel, Kenneth. *Dead Water Zone*. HarperCollins.
Qualey, Marsha. *Thin Ice*. Quercus Press.
* Sacher, Louis. *Holes*. Yearling.
* Spinelli, Jerry. *Wringer*. HarperCollins.
Sweeney, Joyce. *Center Line*. Laurel Leaf.
_____________. *The Tiger Orchard*. Delacorte Books for Young Readers.
Wallace, Bill. *Never Say Quit*. Aladdin.
Wallace, Rich. *Wrestling Sturbridge*. Laurel Leaf.
Westwood, Chris. *Brother of Mine*. Puffin.

Other Books by Edward Bloor

Crusader. Harcourt.
Story Time. Graphia.
Taken. Knopf Books for Young Readers.

* NOVEL-TIES Study Guides are available for these titles.

ANSWER KEY

Part I: Pages 1-33

Vocabulary: 1. c 2. a 3. f 4. b 5. i 6. e 7. h 8. d 9. g; 1. obsessed 2. portable 3. impaired 4. sprinted 5. quarterback 6. sod 7. constitutes 8. dominant 9. penalty

Questions: 1. Paul and his mother had packed up their house in Houston and were about to drive to Tangerine County, Florida to join Mr. Fisher and Paul's brother Erik, who had already been settled there for a week. 2. Paul's recurring memories revealed his distrust and fear of Erik. In one memory, Paul recalled an event when Erik told him his eyes would burst into flames if he looked at the sun through his thick-lensed glasses. In another, a hooded motorist, whom he believed was his brother, attacked him. 3. As Paul and his mother entered Tangerine County, they observed groves of thriving citrus trees, then a wasteland of burning trees, and finally the landscaped lawns and expensive houses of the developments. 4. When his father began talking about the "Erik Fisher Football Dream," Paul tried to change the subject. Failing that, he went to his room. Paul had heard his father indulge in Erik's football dream too many times. 5. Muck fires burned in the fields outside the development because there was lignite in the ground that ignited when lightning struck. Though rain dampened the fires, they continued to smolder, producing smoke that hung over the development. Mrs. Fisher was particularly upset by this news because the Homeowners' Association had neglected to inform the Fishers of the problem when they bought the house. 6. Mike Costello's friendliness, his decency, and the fact that he did not seem to be obsessed with football impressed Paul. 7. Mrs. Fisher was disappointed that Lake Windsor Middle School had no auditorium or gym of its own, and that Paul's classes would be held in portable classrooms situated on a field that flooded during the frequent rainstorms. Paul felt that if the soccer team was decent, he was willing to cope with the school's shortcomings. 8. Paul was confident he would get onto the soccer team because he observed that Joey and his friends were unskilled soccer players. Paul also learned that the position of goaltender would probably be available.

Part 1: Pages 33-61

Vocabulary: 1. torque 2. singed 3. eclipse 4. benefactor 5. perimeter 6. funneling 7. calisthenics 8. slouching

Questions: 1. The story of the eclipse was important to Paul because it explained why his vision was impaired. It also identified him as an example of a child who suffered because he did not follow the advice of adults. The story puzzled Paul because he had no recollection of the event. 2. Paul excused Kerri because he knew he saw well enough to find his classes without her help. He did not wish to draw attention to his impairment. 3. Erik chose Arthur for a friend because he was an untalented player who could not compete with him. Also, Arthur would follow Erik's orders and drive Erik wherever he wished to go. Arthur believed that as Erik's friend, he would be allowed to hold the ball for place kicks. This meant he might receive a small share of Erik's fame and glory. 4. The Homeowners' Association tried to control the appearance of the development by setting standards for consistency and regulating everything from the color of the houses and style of the mailboxes to the landscaping of the yards. Paul's mother never lived in a nice house or neighborhood as a child and appreciated these efforts which protected her investment and kept the development from looking like a "shantytown." 5. Paul theorized that before construction workers leveled the ground to build the development, the site of the Donnellys' house was located on the highest point in the area. The lightning remembered this and continued to strike the area. Joey did not believe lightning was complicated enough to have such awareness. 6. Paul was certain he had landed the job of goalie for the team because he had successfully blocked Tino, the best player on the team, from scoring during practice.7. As a result of Mike Costello's death, Paul's mother held a meeting of football parents to suggest that practice be held at dawn, when the danger from lightning was diminished. Coach Warner opposed this suggestion, stating that players who lived far from the school would not be able to get to practice at that hour. Other parents supported Mrs. Fisher's suggestion and offered to set up a carpool to ensure that all players had transportation to practice.

Part I: Pages 61-94

Vocabulary: 1. obituary 2. eligible 3. migrant 4. osprey 5. elated 6. partitioned 7. commotion 8. vaulting

Questions: 1. Paul blamed his mother when he was dropped from the soccer team because she filled out the forms that identified him as visually impaired. Mrs. Fisher responded to the situation by apologizing to Paul and acknowledging that his visual impairment did not hinder his ability to play soccer well. Mr. Fisher's response was to talk to the coach and relay the suggestion that Paul might be content to act as a manager, rather than a player. 2. Paul was surprised that the conversations at Mike's wake were not about Mike. Instead, people talked about relatively trivial matters, such as the disappearance of the koi from the development's lake. 3. Paul took comfort in the sense of history that the old tangerine packing plant and migrant workers' houses gave to the tangerine groves along Route 22. He imagined that the structure of the packing plant seemed as magnificent to the migrant workers as a European cathedral. He was troubled because these structures were now abandoned and obsolete. 4. Joey hustled Paul away from the boys at the carnival because they were from Tangerine Middle School, where the students had a reputation for running in gangs and carrying guns. 5. Paul didn't go on any of the carnival rides because the rest of the kids ignored him, even Joey. Feeling isolated and alone, Paul chose to wander around on his own. 6. Paul was surprised because the television report minimized the sinkhole disaster. It was reported that the sinkhole was only fifty yards across, and its victims suffered only minor injuries. The report did not capture the horrifying sounds of the wooden walkways cracking and splintering. 7. Mr. Fisher was promoted when it was discovered that his boss, Charley Burns, had been taking bribes from developers, including the developers of Lake Windsor Middle School, in exchange for lax site inspections. Mr. Fisher worried that in his new position he might be "tarred with the same brush" as Charley Burns. 8. Paul was elated because he hoped to transfer to Tangerine Middle School without an IEP, which would give him a second chance to play goalie on a soccer team.

Part 2: Pages 97-124

Vocabulary: 1. vintage – classic; antique 2. vandalism – malicious or ignorant destruction 3. banter – joking; teasing 4. frenzy – frantic outburst of feeling 5. momentum – driving power; thrust

Questions: 1. Paul's visual impairment had always made him feel like an outsider. Since the students at Tangerine Middle School were primarily minority students, Paul felt that he and his fellow students had something in common. 2. Paul was content to play backup for the goalie because he knew that the goalie typically gets injured more often than any other player on the team. With this in mind, he was confident he would get a chance to play in games from time to time. 3. Paul ended his first day at Tangerine Middle School with a sense of hope because his guide Teresa had close connections to the players on the soccer team; his mother "lost" his IEP forms, so he would not be labeled as a handicapped student; and best of all, he had a position on the soccer team. 4. Paul handled Victor's efforts to intimidate him by remaining calm, making a joke at his own expense, and letting Victor know that he was aware of his accomplishments as a soccer player. If Paul had chosen to respond more aggressively, he might have found himself in a fight with Victor, or at least alienated from him and the other players on the soccer team. 5. Joey was disappointed in himself because his fear prevented him from standing up to Eric and Arthur when they made cruel jokes about his brother's death. Paul tried to console Joey by pointing out that it was the boys' behavior that was cowardly, not Joey's response. Paul assured Joey that Erik and Arthur were not worth agonizing over. 6. The War Eagles were a better team than the Palmetto Whippoorwills because they were more skilled, focused, and disciplined. The War Eagles played the game as a team, while the Whippoorwills only had a few talented players whom they relied on to intimidate opposing teams. 7. Victor apologized to Paul for yelling at him and told him that he appreciated his efforts during the game. Victor also told Paul that being a War Eagle meant playing to the fullest. As a committed teammate, Paul essentially became a member of a family that would back him up and protect him.

Part 2: Pages 124-155

Vocabulary: Across — 1. dilapidated 4. swiveled 6. adjourn 8. fumigate 9. condemned; Down — 2. initiation 3. decoy 4. sulking 5. prominence 7. punt

Questions: 1. Eric's parents tried to relieve the humiliation of the fake kick by reminding Eric that it played a key role in winning the game. When his pratfall appeared on the evening news, his parents tried to make light of it, urging him to put the incident behind him. 2. When Paul watched Shandra play goalie, he was impressed by how sharp and big she looked, like an American Gladiator. By comparison, he felt he must look small and goofy with his goggles. 3. Victor was taken out of the game with Kinnow when an old cut over his eye opened up and needed to be stitched. He helped his teammates to victory by reminding them how much they wanted to win, and by leading them in a unifying war chant that sent them onto the field with a renewed sense of determination and comradeship. 4. Paul was shocked when he scored a goal because he had never done it before. 5. Maya was confused by Mrs. Fisher's words of encouragement because she was already the top scoring player in the county and was assured of making the All-County Team. 6. Joey turned down Mrs. Fisher's invitation because he did not want another encounter with Erik and Arthur. Paul compared the fumigated atmosphere in Joey's house with the cruelty and denial that poisoned his own home. 7. Paul learned that Joey was prejudiced when Joey referred to the students at Tangerine Middle School as natives in the jungle. Paul later recalled a conversation in which Joey referred to Theresa as a "guide dog." 8. The Homeowners'

Association had tried to extinguish the muck fires by flooding them. These efforts proved unsuccessful not only because they failed to put out the fires, but also because the swamps they created provided a breeding ground for an infestation of mosquitoes.

Part 2: Pages 155-199

Vocabulary: 1. congregated 2. scion 3. boycott 4. peripheral 5. cleats 6. reverence 7. retaliate 8. horticulture

Questions: 1. Paul was worried about seeing Tino because he was afraid Tino might blame him, as well as Joey, for his suspension from school. Paul won Tino's respect by helping at the tangerine nursery and by confessing that it was he who informed on Tino and his friends after the incident at the carnival. 2. Termites were infesting the housing development because it was built over tangerine trees that were burned and plowed under. The termites lived in the underground wood. They infested the houses when they came up to the surface for water. Fumigation was a temporary remedy because it only provided a barrier; it did not destroy the termites living underground. 3. The billowing cloud of mosquito spray jogged Paul's memory back to a time in the backyard of his former home when his father was testing his peripheral vision. 4. Paul believed he could "see" better than his parents because he was aware of Erik's duplicity while they were not. He regarded Erik's status as a football hero as a facade that concealed a ruthless predator. 5. Paul felt his season with the War Eagles was the greatest thing that ever happened to him because he was part of a team that was feared by its opponents. Paul had never before been on the intimidating side of fear. 6. Tino revered his brother Luis, while Paul feared and loathed his brother Erik. 7. The Tangerine War Eagles regarded the Lake Windsor soccer team as its archenemy because the War Eagles had lost the championship to them last year in a home game. Victor had been particularly insulted when a player on the Lake Windsor team mocked the War Eagles. 8. According to Paul, his soccer teammates were only impressed with the housing developments because they didn't realize that their perceived luxury and grandeur was superficial. 9. Though Victor was assaulted and had to be taken out of the game, Coach Bright refocused her team by reminding them that they were there to play soccer. If they sought retaliation, they would be playing the other team's game, rather than their own.

Part 3: Pages 203-230

Vocabulary: 1. f 2. d 3. a 4. g 5. c 6. e 7. b; 1. debris 2. paralyzed 3. trudge 4. insolent 5. rickety 6. mesmerized 7. contorted

Questions: 1. Erik assaulted Tino because he responded to Erik's insults with mocking remarks. Unable to bully or humiliate Tino, Erik lost control and lashed out violently against him. 2. Arthur, who acted as Erik's bodyguard, clubbed Luis who had come to the football field to confront Erik after his brother Tino had been assaulted. 3. Students from families that owned agricultural businesses were absent from school during the freeze because they were needed at home to help their families save their crops. 4. Luis sprayed water over the trees so it would ice, encasing them and keeping their temperature from dropping below thirty-two degrees. 5. Luis hesitated to accept Paul's help because he wondered why Erik Fisher's brother would want to help. Paul convinced Luis of his good will by saying he was a War Eagle, someone who helped out his teammates on and off the field. 6. Though the "lightning trees" were dead, the Cruz family avoided chopping them down because they stood on the highest ground and served as lightning rods. They did chop down a few of them during the freeze because they needed them for firewood. 7. People in Lake Windsor Downs responded to the freeze by welcoming it with hot cocoa, fake logs, and Christmas CDs. In contrast, the people of Tangerine had to fight the freeze with shovels, axes, and fire if their livelihoods were to be protected.

Part 3: Pages 230-265

Vocabulary: 1. mirage 2. bogus 3. veered 4. prostrate 5. sterile 6. pummeling

Questions: 1. Mr. Fisher had deleted from the file all those colleges that were considered noncontenders for the national title: they did not support his ambitions for Erik's football career. 2. The freeze killed off the mosquitoes and may have killed the termites, as well. This meant that the fumigating and spraying could stop. 3. Paul resisted sharing his suspicions with his mother because he was unsure of her response. He feared she would simply dismiss his suspicions as she always had and assume they were simply a by-product of his illness. 4. Paul was sure Erik and Arthur were responsible for Luis's death after he contacted the county medical center. From the nurse at the center, he learned that a blow to the head could cause an aneurysm to burst, even several days after the blow was delivered. 5. Luis's family knew the truth about his death because Luis told his family members about his encounter with Erik and Arthur. Their understanding of the truth seemed mysterious to Paul because he had never experienced family life in which everyone shared the same version of the truth. 6. When Erik and Arthur threatened Paul with the baseball bat, he was unafraid because they seemed lame and pathetic. Inspired by Luis's example, Paul stood up to the bullies and used his own powerful weapon—the truth about Luis's death. 7. Paul's parents had lied to him about the true cause of his visual impairment because they had hoped he would never remember the incident. They did not want him to grow up hating his brother. Paul convinced them that this was a terrible decision when he pointed out that by avoiding the truth, they had created a false history that caused Paul to hate himself.

Part 3: Pages 266-303

Vocabulary: 1. c 2. f 3. b 4. g 5. e 6. d 7. h 8. a; 1. meekly 2. ransacked 3. nullify 4. curtly 5. immortality 6. unanimous 7. compelled 8. restitution

Questions: 1. Antoine knew that Paul witnessed Luis's murder. He was urging Paul to step forward and tell the truth. Paul was startled, and assumed Antoine was going to make a statement about Luis's death to the Sheriff's Department. 2. Antoine's confession caused the Tangerine County Sports Commission to decide that he was not a legitimate member of the Lake Windsor High School football team. Because of this, all victories in which Antoine was involved were nullified. All other records set by team members were erased as well, including Erik's records for longest field goal, highest field-goal percentages in a season, and most extra points in a season. This represented the end of Erik's football dream. 3. Antoine initially chose to lie about where he lived because if he had played football at Tangerine High, no important scouts would ever have come to see him play, and his chances of advancing his football career would have been greatly diminished. 4. Mr. Donnelly knew that he retained his record because of a technicality. He also knew that Antoine was a more accomplished player than he had been. 5. Paul was trying to make the point that Mr. Fisher, Coach Warner, Mr. Bridge, and others in their community must have had something wrong with their eyesight because they did not see the truth of a situation (i.e., Antoine didn't live in the school district) if it worked against their desires. On the other hand, Paul, who was visually impaired, saw the truth because he did not shut his eyes to it. 6. Mrs. Fisher called a meeting at her house on behalf of the Fisher and Baver families in order to return all of the items that Erik and Arthur had stolen from homes that had been tented and evacuated for pesticide spraying. 7. Mr. Fisher wanted unanimous agreement to the restitution plan because it was a condition for the police to drop charges against Erik and Arthur. 8. Paul's grandparents weren't surprised about Erik's violence because they had been aware of it ever since he assaulted his brother. They had strongly and persistently advised Erik's parents to get professional help for their son. 9. Paul knew he would go to St. Anthony's with his new reputation as a "bad dude" who got expelled from every public school in Tangerine County. This would earn him a fearful respect from his new classmates. 10. Paul revealed the complete truth about his actions at the award ceremony in a disk that he provided for the police. Answers to the second part of the question will vary.

Notes: